Zinger Bug Zoe

Living with Autism

by
Gayle L. Betz

Illustrations by
Dawn Baumer

AuthorHouse™
1663 Liberty Drive
Bloomington, IN 47403
www.authorhouse.com
Phone: 1 (833) 262-8899

Because of the dynamic nature of the Internet, any web addresses or links contained in this book may have changed since publication and may no longer be valid. The views expressed in this work are solely those of the author and do not necessarily reflect the views of the publisher, and the publisher hereby disclaims any responsibility for them.

Any people depicted in stock imagery provided by Getty Images are models, and such images are being used for illustrative purposes only.
Certain stock imagery © Getty Images.

This book is printed on acid-free paper.

First published by AuthorHouse 09/12/2006

ISBN: 978-1-4259-5963-0 (sc)
ISBN: 978-1-4817-2713-6 (e)

Print information available on the last page.

Published by AuthorHouse 10/07/2020

author HOUSE®

For my daughter Zoe, whose strength and determination, through many challenges has been my inspiration.

And, for Kerstyn Green, the awesome woman who opened doors for Zoe, and patiently waited for her to pass through.

Zinger Bug Zoe is my name
and you can plainly see.

I look like all the other
beetlebugs in Tweedledee!

Yet, deep inside my little bod
a "zingy" feeling sits.

If someone touches me or talks,
I have a zinger fit!

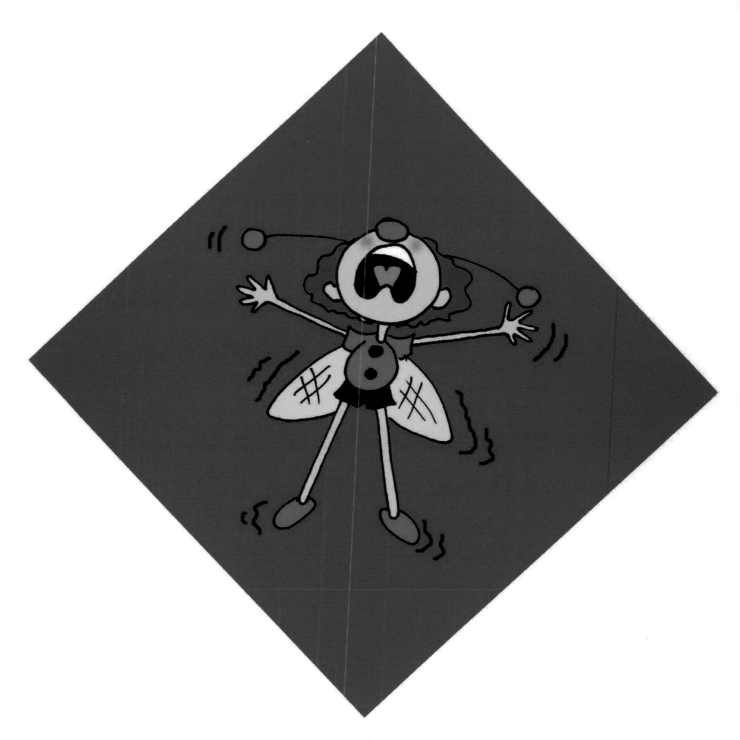

It isn't something that I want,
the feelings just come out.

And, there are times that I
can't do anything but shout.

It makes me sad
cuz I want friends
the way the others do.

But, I can really scare
those friends if hollering
comes through.

I try my best to hold it in,
with excitement at its peak.
But there are times,
even with that;
I must let out a squeak.

Mom and my siblings try their best
to help me, and they pray.
But, thank GOD for my teacher
the very precious Kerstyn Kay.

**Miss Kerstyn is my buddy and
though she can be tough,
I know for sure she loves me and
will push me just enough...**

...to control my many "zinger fits"
that want to pop right out.
For, I can't be in public,
if all I do is shout.

So, as I grow I want to thank
my teacher every day---SO MUCH!

For now I've learned to listen
and to even handle touch!

I've learned to cope when
"zinger" feelings show up;
and they do.

"A friend loveth at all times"
Proverbs 17:17a

But with help
from friends and family,
great happiness
shines through!

Zinger Bug Zoe would like you to know some things about Autism.

- A gentle touch can feel like needles poking Zoe's skin.

- Sounds that other people might ignore can hurt Zoe's ears.

- Certain lights can really sting her eyes.

- Being different is o.k. but Zoe needs friends, too.

Can you be one?

Printed in the United States
By Bookmasters

Author pictured with daughter Zoe

Gayle Betz is a Preschool Teacher and mother of five, living in Michigan. She has been a Parent Advocate for many years as a result of having two children with developmental disabilities, Autism and Cerebral Palsy Quadriplegia. Gayle is currently writing a series of books for young children to help them create a positive attitude towards identifying differences and individuality in people with disabilities.

ISBN 978-1-4259-5963-0

51999

9 781425 959630

Betty Gets Ready...
For School

Written and Illustrated by Kathi Greene